NEW KID

NEW KID NEW SCENE

A Guide to Moving and Switching Schools

**by Debbie Glasser, PhD
and Emily Schenck**

Magination Press • Washington, DC
American Psychological Association

Published by
MAGINATION PRESS
An Educational Publishing Foundation Book
American Psychological Association
750 First Street, NE
Washington, DC 20002

For more information about our books, including a complete catalog, please write to us, call 1-800-374-2721, or visit our website at www.apa.com/pubs/magination.

Book design by Naylor Design, Inc., Washington, DC
Printed by Worzalla, Stevens Point, Wisconsin

Library of Congress Cataloging-in-Publication Data
Glasser, Debbie.
  New kid, new scene : a guide to moving and switching schools / by Debbie Glasser and Emily Schenck.
     p. cm.
  "American Psychological Association."
  ISBN-13: 978-1-4338-1039-8 (hardcover)
  ISBN-10: 1-4338-1039-5 (hardcover)
  ISBN-13: 978-1-4338-1038-1 (pbk.)
  ISBN-10: 1-4338-1038-7 (pbk.)
  1. Students, Transfer of—United States—Psychological aspects—Juvenile literature.
2. Transfer students—United States—Psychology—Juvenile literature. 3. Moving, Household—Juvenile literature. 4. Moving, Household—Psychological aspects—Juvenile literature. 5. Moving, Household—Social aspects—Juvenile literature. 6. Children—Life skills guides—Juvenile literature. 7. Children—United States—Social life and customs—Juvenile literature. I. Schenck, Emily. II. American Psychological Association. III. Title.
  LB3064.2.G57 2012
  373.18—dc22
                                                              2011013608

Manufactured in the United States of America
10 9 8 7 6 5 4 3 2 1

CONTENTS

INTRODUCTION

Preparing for Your New Role as the New Kid

You probably didn't audition for a part in a Hollywood movie, but if you're new to a school, home, neighborhood—or maybe all three—you may feel like you've just been given the starring role in a film about someone else's life.

Act One. The camera focuses on you walking through the halls of school. As you look around, you see colorful artwork and posters hanging on the walls. Guys and girls are rushing to class before the bell rings. Pizza is being served in the cafeteria. "These props look familiar," you think to yourself. "But, something doesn't feel quite right." That's because those aren't your colorful posters. That's not your cafeteria. And those certainly aren't your friends sitting in the lunchroom.

Act Two. The school bus doors close behind you. It was filled with kids you've never seen before. You walk down the street and put your key in the door of the blue and white house on the corner. It has a mailbox, a driveway, and a big tree in the yard—just like your old house—but somehow, things don't feel like home.

Act Three. The camera zooms in for a close-up of your bewildered face. "Now what?" you wonder, as you frantically try to think of your next line.

"Cut!" yells the director.

If you've been feeling like an actor on a movie set—without a script, a director, or a clue about how your story is going to unfold—you must be a new kid.

Then . . . and Now

Before you switched schools or moved to a new town, you probably recognized most of the faces in the hall as you walked to math class. You knew all the words to your school song. You also knew which radio station played your favorite music, where to buy your favorite fruit smoothie, and which friend to sit with in the lunchroom.

Now, the faces and places in your life are new, different, and unfamiliar. You have to figure out how to feel at home, how to fit in, and how to be yourself. You may feel out of place or uncertain sometimes. There's a chance you may also be curious—and even a little excited—about what's ahead.

You're not the only person to deal with these mixed emotions and wonder, "Whose life am I living?" In fact, there's a large cast of characters—kids just like you—who've been there, too.

New kid

(noun): a terrific guy or girl who is still the same person, but is now living in a new house, going to a new school, or experiencing some sort of new situation that just doesn't feel familiar.

Meet Some Cast Members

Yasmin

Character traits: Hard-working, creative, and a little shy.

Story line: Yasmin was in the fifth grade when she decided to apply to a performing arts middle school. When she received her acceptance letter, she felt happy and proud. Dancing is Yasmin's passion, and she couldn't wait for the first day of school.

Plot twist: The day before school started, Yasmin started sweating and felt a knot in the middle of her stomach. Her friends were getting ready to start the sixth grade at their neighborhood school, but Yasmin would be starting the performing arts school on her own. "I was afraid my old friends would make new friends, and I would have to be by myself and wouldn't have anyone to talk to," she says.

Hannah

Character traits: Talkative, outgoing, and adventurous.

Story line: After living in the same town for 14 years, Hannah and her family moved to a new state so they could live closer to grandparents, aunts, uncles, and cousins. Hannah was curious about other parts of the country. She wondered what it would be like to live somewhere new. Also, Hannah was close with her relatives and wanted to be near them.

Plot twist: Although Hannah describes herself as adventurous, she was facing a lot of changes at once. Not only was she

9

starting a new school in a new town, she had to say goodbye to her best friend, Julia. Hannah and Julia had met in elementary school, and they spent time together almost every weekend. They even went to the same summer camp and talked about going to the same college one day. Now, Hannah was moving away. "When I told Julia I was moving, she got mad at me and I didn't know what to do," Hannah says.

James

Character traits: Athletic, funny, and friendly.

Story line: James was 11 years old when his family moved more than 2,000 miles away to another part of the country. He used to live in a warm climate where temperatures rarely dipped below 75 degrees. Then, in December, he and his family moved to a small mountain town that can get up to 90 inches of snow every year.

Plot twist: In his old neighborhood, James played sports in the street with his friends almost every day after school. When he walked out the front door, there was always some-one around for a game of football, kickball, or baseball. In his new hometown, there were very few kids on the block and very few houses nearby. There were no football games being played in the street. In fact, there wasn't even an actual street! His new home was perched on a winding road made of dirt, not asphalt. James wondered if he'd ever be able to enjoy his favorite activity again. What's more, because he was living in the mountains, he had to think about things he never worried about before—like what to wear in a place with cold weather, ice, and

snow. "When I moved, everything changed, even my clothes," he explains.

Stay Tuned

If you're curious about what happens in their next scenes, stay tuned! You'll read more about these star characters' twists and turns. In the meantime, here's a sneak preview: Yasmin still had first-day jitters, but met a new friend by the end of the week. Hannah and Julia survived a rocky patch in their friendship and are still making summer plans together. James's passion for athletics led him to a new sport he'd never tried before, and his sense of humor helped him meet new friends on a neighborhood team.

Of course, not all "new kid" situations have Hollywood endings. It's not always easy to make new friends, keep old ones, fit in, and feel at home. James, for example, still misses his friends from the old neighborhood. He also wishes he had more kids nearby to play ball with. Although Yasmin made new friends at the performing arts school, she did lose touch with some of her old friends because she doesn't see them as often as she used to. Even Hannah and Julia's relationship isn't what it used to be. They each have new best friends, and don't text each other or visit as often as they had planned.

Most new kids agree that, in time—and with support and helpful advice—you won't feel like the new kid for long, and you won't be dealing with new-kid issues forever. Even though your world may feel like it's turned around, hang in there! Soon, you'll go from being the new kid to being one of the kids.

In this book, you'll get plenty of tips and advice from a great cast of characters who know how it feels to face new-kid challenges. The guys and girls we interviewed range in age from 8–14. They've experienced all kinds of situations—from tough to terrific. Each of them walked down unfamiliar halls or slept in an unfamiliar room, and now feels at home.

In fact, every year, millions of kids change their schools and their scenery. Like you, they face all kinds of challenging situations and wonder, "How will I handle this?" However, they also experience plenty of times when they feel grateful for their new experiences and say, "How amazing is this!?"

Stage Fright

Although being a new kid does have plenty of perks (like the chance to meet new people and learn new things—to name a few), even the most adventurous guy or girl can break out in a cold sweat just thinking about facing an unfamiliar situation. In fact, most new kids worry about feeling alone or left out. They also stress about things like where to sit during lunch or on the school bus when there's not a familiar face in sight.

Before the curtain goes up in any performance, it's normal to get a little stage fright. Here are some common new-kid worries expressed by guys and girls we interviewed for this book:

* I don't know anyone and I'm not sure how to meet new friends.

* I won't have anyone to sit with in the lunchroom.

* My old friends will forget about me.

* The kids I meet aren't going to be friendly.

* I won't know my way around my neighborhood or my school, and might get lost.

* Things won't feel like home.

Whether you're starting a new school without your old friends or moving to a new town, you probably feel uncertain about what to expect. You may also feel unprepared about what to do next.

How to Use This Book

It's important to remember that new kids aren't new kids for long. Before you know it, you'll be busy hanging with friends and living life in your new place. In the meantime, we wrote this book to help kids (just like you) feel more comfortable and confident playing the part of the new kid. Starting a new chapter in life isn't something you do every day. You probably have plenty of questions about what to do and say so you can make the most of all the changes.

In each chapter, you'll find **Casting Calls.** These are fun charts and quizzes to help you learn new things about yourself and your character—like what you really want in a friend, and how you handle new situations. Also, you'll see **What's My Next Line?** boxes throughout the book. These will help you learn what you can do when things don't go as planned, or when you're having a tough time. Each chapter also includes lots of fun tips to help you enjoy your starring role as the new kid.

In this book, you'll learn:

✳ How to meet new friends in—and out of—school

✳ How to juggle old and new friendships

✳ How to survive the first day in a new school

✳ How (and why) to put your best foot forward in a new place

* How to enjoy your own company (and even your little brother's) while waiting for your social life to develop

* How to fit in—without barging in—on established friendships

* . . . and more!

Because everyone's personality and experiences are unique, there's no such thing as a movie script for the new kid. This book won't tell you exactly what to say or when to say it in every new-kid situation. That wouldn't be realistic, or much fun. Instead, you'll learn new ideas and useful suggestions to help you feel more comfortable and confident.

You can read this book from cover to cover, or just skim it and read a little at a time. Not all the situations described in this book will be exactly like yours. For example, you may attend a new school, but still live in the same house. On the other hand, you may have moved to another country where people speak a different language and drive on the other side of the road. Either way, this book can help you learn a lot about how to handle the many changes in your life.

Now, the curtain is about to go up and you're getting ready for action. Keep reading to learn how to make the most of your move, and enjoy your new role.

CHAPTER 1

Making Your Move

> I applied to a performing arts school and got in. I didn't know anyone who was going there, so I was nervous. I was also happy because I love to dance and they have a really good program.
>
> **—Yasmin, 11**

> I remember the night we actually moved. I didn't know what to expect.
>
> **—Janessa, 12**

> I was kind of excited because I had never moved before. Besides, I hated the cold weather and thought it would be fun to live in the south.
>
> **—Calvin, 12**

Like Janessa, Calvin, and Yasmin, you probably have all kinds of feelings, too. You may be excited one day, and sad, worried, or angry the next. On one hand, you might be happy about the opportunity to experience something new, like a warmer winter or a really interesting school. On the other hand, you may feel sad or mad about all the changes you're going through, like leaving friends or familiar surroundings. You may also feel nervous about what to expect.

Here's the good news: These feelings are normal.

Now, here's more good news: You're not alone. Each year, many kids just like you move to a new home, start a new school, or experience another big change in their lives.

"Fine," you say. "So I'm not the only one with a million thoughts whirling around in my head. Now what?"

We're glad you asked! In this chapter you'll learn how to sort through what's on your mind and deal with common new-kid worries.

Worries and Wishes

Being a new kid means you're experiencing changes in your life. Even though these changes will likely bring positive experiences your way, it's normal to worry a little—or even a lot—about what's next. In fact, your mind might be filled with worries and wishes. Sharing these feelings with parents and other trusted people in your life can be a great way to gather more information about what to expect and start to feel better.

Worries

Luke was nine when his family moved to a new town and he started a new school. When he first heard he'd be moving, these are the three things he said he worried about most:

1. I was afraid my teacher would ask me for my address and I wouldn't remember it, and then I'd embarrass myself in front of the class.

2. I was afraid I'd forget how to get to my classroom or I'd get on the wrong bus.

3. I was afraid to meet new people. I didn't know if they'd be weird.

What are your three biggest worries? Grab a piece of paper and a pen, or open up a new document on a computer, and put your worries in writing.

Wishes

Eleven-year-old Gianna wasn't happy when her mom announced that she and her sister would be transferring to a new middle school without their old friends. "We were upset, at first, because we didn't know what to expect. Would we make new friends? Would we stay close with our old ones? Would the work be really hard?" she recalls. Gianna and her sister weren't the only ones who felt upset. "Our friends were hurt. They felt like we were leaving them," she says. Before the first day of school, these were her three biggest wishes:

1. I wished I could keep all of my old friends.

2. I wished I could meet a new friend on the first day of school so I wouldn't have to sit by myself in class or at lunch.

3 I wished I knew how hard the homework was going to be and whether I could handle it.

Now, it's your turn. If you had a new-kid wish list, what would you wish for? Add your wishes, in writing, to the list you've already begun.

Sometimes, it feels good just to think about what and how you are feeling and write it down. Other times, though, it's helpful to share what you're feeling with someone you trust—like a parent or grandparent. That's what Luke did. He told his mom what he was worrying about. "She said the teacher already had my address in the front office and probably wouldn't ask me for it in front of the other kids," Luke explains. "She also helped me memorize our address and phone number so I wouldn't worry about forgetting them."

Luke's mom also came up with an idea to help him feel less stressed about getting lost. She wrote his bus number on a piece of paper and put it in his backpack. She also arranged for a tour of the school so Luke could find his homeroom class.

My old school was small and there was only one hall. In my new school, there were lots of halls. I was so nervous I would walk into the wrong classroom. For the first few days, I asked teachers in the hall where I should go. They always pointed me in the right direction!

—Pilar, 11

Gianna's biggest wish was to keep her old friends. She decided to share these feelings with her friends by explaining that, even though she was changing schools, she didn't want to lose their friendships. She managed to stay close with some of her old friends, and also made plenty of new ones. You'll learn more about how kids like Gianna juggle old and new friendships in Chapter 7.

Gianna was also eager to meet new friends quickly. She didn't want to sit alone on the first day of school. As it turns out, kids were given assigned seats—in class and in the lunchroom—at Gianna's new middle school. She decided to introduce herself to the people sitting next to her and said things like, "Hi, I'm Gianna. I'm new here. What can you tell me about the after-school sports and clubs?"

Even though assigned seating didn't produce an instant best friend, Gianna was able to enjoy some friendly conversations with the guys and girls sitting near her. What's more, she didn't have to spend the entire lunch period staring at the "Eat Your Veggies" poster on the wall. Eventually, Gianna made a number of close friends who share more in common with her than a seat assignment (you'll learn how in Chapter 5). Now, when she walks the halls of her new school, she sees plenty of familiar people who smile and wave.

Another common wish is to have some sort of ability to see into the future. It's normal to want to know what to expect in a new situation. That's what Luke wished for when he worried whether the kids in his new town would somehow be strange or mean. Gianna also wished for her own crystal ball. She wanted to know that she'd be able to handle the homework at her new school, which had a reputation for being challenging and competitive.

Of course, it's impossible to look into the future. However, you can feel better about the present *and* the future by doing what Luke and Gianna did. They expressed their fears, gathered some facts, and sought some friendly advice. A lot of kids have probably faced the same fears you might have. Here are some that may seem familiar, along with some facts, and advice from real kids who have moved or switched schools.

Fears, Facts, and Friendly Advice

Fear
What if no one likes me?

Fact
This is a common concern. In fact, most new kids admit they worry about this when they start a new school, join a new club, or move to a new town. Just for fun, let's take a look at the facts from an historical point of view. Have you had friends in the past? If you answered "yes" to this question, there's no reason why you won't have friends in the future.

Friendly Advice
Aaron, who started a new school at age 10, had this fear, too. Here's what he says: "Everyone has something about him or her that's interesting to others. It may take a little time, but you'll definitely find people who like you for you."

Fear
What if everyone's weird?

Fact
Unless you're moving to another planet, kids will be kids wherever you go! Some may speak with an accent you've

> I was worried and surprised when my parents told me we were moving, but I knew I'd have them with me.
>
> —Liu, 8

never heard before. Others may wear different types of clothes than you do. Kids in different parts of the country may even enjoy eating foods you've never tried. However, these differences don't make them weird. In fact, they probably make the people you meet more interesting.

Friendly Advice

What you may really be wondering is, "Will I have things in common with the new kids I meet?" and "Will I fit in?" Janessa, who was 12 when she moved to a new state, says, "Hang in there. The answer to these questions is definitely yes!"

Fear

What if I have no one to sit with at lunch?

Fact

Ah, the lunch question. This is something almost every new kid worries about. That's because lunch is a very social time during the school day. Many new kids worry that they'll feel left out or lonely if they don't have anyone to sit with or talk to in the lunchroom. It can be scary to take that first step and introduce yourself to others. There may be times when you say hi to someone, sit with him or her at lunch, and still feel like you're strangers. Remember that new friendships take time to grow. Also, you may discover that you don't have much in common with one person, but you have plenty of things in common with someone else. Keep your eyes open for new people to talk to in your classes, the lunchroom, or on the bus. If you're having a tough time meeting new people, share your feelings with an adult you trust, like a parent or teacher.

Friendly Advice

Hannah, who moved to a new state when she was 14, says, "First of all, it's really okay if you don't have someone to sit with the first few days of school. You can't rush friendships. But if you aren't comfortable sitting on your own, it's also okay to go up to someone who was in one of your classes and say, 'Hi, can I sit here?' Most people will say 'yes.' If they don't, you probably wouldn't want to be their friend anyway."

Fear

What if I lose my old friends?

Fact

In a survey of over 1,200 kids, SmartGirl.org asked the question, "If your best friend moved really far from you, how do you (or would you) keep in touch?" Almost half of those who responded said they'd stay connected through e-mails and instant messages. About a third said they'd keep in contact with phone calls. Others said they'd send letters or visit. Fewer than 2 percent of kids said they'd do nothing at all to stay close to an old friend.

Friendly Advice

"There are lots of ways to keep in touch with your old friends," says Hannah. "Text, call, or e-mail when you can." That's what Hannah did. She also sent her best friend fun packages, like leaves during the fall and a t-shirt from her new school.

Hannah adds, "Even though you'll probably talk to your old friends a lot in the beginning, you may not stay close with every one of them. But you'll always stay in touch with the people you care the most about." That's what Hannah did with her best friend. They still talk and visit each other when they can.

Fear

What if the work is much harder at my new school?

Fact

Many kids discover that the assignments and tests in their new school seem similar to the ones at their old school. However, some kids find that the work is much easier—or harder. Your new math teacher might be covering topics that you've already learned, yet your new English teacher might be assigning long chapter books, even though you used to read short essays in your last English class. If you feel a little ahead in some classes and a little behind in others, this is common! However, if you're feeling far behind the other kids in any of your classes, it's important to share this with a parent, teacher, or counselor so you can get extra support to help make your new classes easier to manage.

Friendly Advice

Gabriel was 11 when he started a new school that was known for having challenging classes. He says he had to learn a whole new way of studying. "I couldn't wait until the last minute like I used to!" he explains. "My teachers were really helpful. They gave us tips on how to study and answered questions when we needed help."

Sad Feelings

Even if you're less worried about what to expect in your new situation, you may still be sad or even mad about all the changes in your life. Share these emotions with your parents. You might say, "I'm sad that we're moving. Can we talk about it?"

That's what Nick did. He was 10 when his family moved. It was their third move to a new state. "I kept telling my parents, 'I don't want to move again. I just made friends in my new school and now I have to start all over,'" he explains. "I let it out by talking to a lot of people, like my parents and grandparents. My parents kept saying that they'll help me, and that things will get better. Now I love it here!"

There may be times when you'll feel better by sharing your thoughts with family members or friends. However, there may be other times when you might still be worried, angry, or sad. These experiences might even be getting in the way of doing things you usually enjoy. It's important to talk with a trusted adult in your life to let him or her know that you're experiencing these big feelings. Help is available! Your parents might make an appointment for you to talk with a professional (like a psychologist) who is specially trained to help kids handle difficult situations. Reaching out for help is an

more

important step in learning how to cope with all the changes in your life.

From time to time, kids (and adults!) need extra help figuring out their emotions and handling difficult situations. That's when they might see a psychologist. Psychologists are professionals who have special training to understand people's emotions, and help them cope with tough times and feel better. Psychologists want to help kids deal with big emotions and find helpful solutions to challenges.

If you meet with a psychologist, he or she will talk with you to understand your feelings and your experiences. The psychologist will also want to talk with your parents to get a better understanding of what's going on and how they can help. Many times, psychologists who work with kids have art supplies and games in their office to help you feel comfortable and offer various ways to express yourself and your emotions. Talking with a psychologist is meant to be a positive experience. Seeing a psychologist can be a helpful and meaningful way to work out solutions to difficult situations and feel better.

> I met with a counselor to talk about my feelings. She was really nice and helped me feel a lot better.
>
> —Aaron, 10

Plot Summary

In this chapter, you learned that making a move can spark all kinds of worries and wishes. You learned the importance of expressing your fears and reaching out to others for help, information, and support. You also learned that many of the things you were scared about might not be so scary, after all.

 ## Coming Attractions

Are you wondering whether you'll ever feel comfortable in your new situation? Learn how to create a first-class comfort zone in Chapter Two.

CHAPTER 2

Getting Comfortable When You're Not in Your Comfort Zone

> It was strange to be in a school where I didn't know anyone. I didn't know the teachers or the kids. I didn't know where anything was. I didn't know anything.
>
> **—James, 11**

> When we first moved in, it was really weird waking up in my new room. I didn't know where I was.
>
> **—Hannah, 14**

hen James first started his new school, he felt confused and out of place. When Hannah woke up in her new room, she felt the same way. Hannah and James discovered they were no longer in their comfort zones.

What Is a Comfort Zone?

A "comfort zone" isn't necessarily a specific place. It's actually a term used to describe the feeling you get when you're happy and comfortable in a situation—whatever or wherever that situation is. No two comfort zones are exactly alike. In fact, you may have a very different comfort zone than your brother or your best friend.

For James, it was how he felt in his old school. That's where he could walk through the halls and recognize every face. It was also the place where he could easily find his seat in the lunchroom—right next to his best friend. Things seemed familiar. James was in control. He didn't worry that he might accidentally call someone the wrong name, or that he'd walk into the gym instead of the bathroom. James was in his comfort zone.

Hannah felt most comfortable when she was in her bedroom. That's where she could relax, connect with her friends on the computer, flip through the pages of a magazine, and listen to her favorite music—all at the same time. Even though her room was usually a mess, Hannah never seemed to have trouble finding what she needed. Math notes from last Tuesday? They were probably under the bed. Last season's recording of her favorite reality TV show? It was in the closet behind her soccer cleats. In her room, everything seemed familiar. Hannah was in control. She didn't worry that she might not be able to find her favorite country music CD or recognize the view out her window. Hannah was in her comfort zone.

You may have felt like you were in your comfort zone while walking through the halls of your old school, sleeping in your old bedroom, or eating your favorite dessert at your old kitchen table. Now, those places have changed and you're probably wondering if you'll ever be in your comfort zone again.

Hang in there. Help is on the way! Since a comfort zone doesn't have to be an actual place (it's often described as a feeling), you can find your zone wherever you are. Learning to be comfortable in a new situation is a great skill to have—not just now, but as you get older—because life is filled with new situations and experiences.

Create Your Comfort Zone

Since everyone's comfort zone is unique, only you can pinpoint exactly what helps you feel comfortable. So let's get started. Grab a pen and paper, or open a new document on your computer, and make a list of the things that may help you find your comfort zone.

Your list might look like this:

* My slightly falling-apart stuffed animal that I sleep with every night.

* The picture of my best friend and me at summer camp.

* My goldfish, Frank, that I won at the fifth grade carnival.

* A quiet place to watch my favorite movies without being interrupted by my little brother.

* My favorite sports equipment so I can play wherever I am.

* A parent or grandparent I can talk to about all the changes in my life.

Now, go ahead and list your comfort zone needs. Be sure to share these with your parents so you can work together to create a new comfort zone that feels right for you.

Getting comfortable in a new situation may take a little time, but it does happen. According to James and Hannah, it may happen sooner than you think, especially if you try some of the *find-your-comfort-zone* ideas that worked for them.

Three Things James Did to Feel More Comfortable in His New School

1 **Check it out.** Before James's first day of school, his parents arranged for a tour with the guidance counselor. That way, he could practice walking to his classes, and locate the lunchroom, the bathrooms, and the bus loop. That early look helped the school seem a little more familiar to James. On his first day of school, James's guidance counselor introduced him to a few students through their student ambassador program. These students walked with James to some classes and even sat with him during lunch. After a few conversations, James already felt a little more at ease.

When I switched to a new school, I met with a tour guide who explained some things to me, but I still felt like I didn't know what was going on. I kept asking questions until I felt more comfortable.

—Angie, 12

2 **Wear something old.** That's right! Before you ask your parents for an increase in your allowance to replace your entire wardrobe, you might want to save that money for new books or a video game. Even though it can be fun to buy new clothes and carry a new backpack at the start of a new school year, James decided he'd seen enough new things lately. So instead of walking into an unfamiliar place wearing unfamiliar clothes, he chose to wear his favorite (and slightly torn) basketball jersey on the first day of his new school. He also held on to the backpack he used last year. That way, he knew exactly where to store his phone so it wouldn't break when he let his backpack fall to the floor next to his desk.

3 **Ask.** Even with a tour, James still had trouble finding all his classrooms during the first few days of school—especially when there were tons of students crowding the halls. So he decided to ask others for directions. "Let people show you around," James suggests. "Most people are nice enough to say, 'Yeah, I can show you.' Besides, it can be a good way to meet people without having to think of things to talk about." Instead of asking another student, you might prefer to ask a teacher for directions or simply study a map of the school. That's okay! Make the choice that feels most comfortable for you.

Three Things Hannah Did to Feel More Comfortable in Her New Room

1 **Re-decorate.** Even though Hannah loved her old room, she didn't necessarily love the pastel colored walls or the teddy bear bedspread she got for her sixth birthday. So she asked her parents if it would be okay to make some changes in her new room. Hannah and her mom went to the paint store together and chose a dark blue hue for her walls. They also picked out a brightly colored comforter and some neon orange pillows. Although the new room didn't feel like her old one, Hannah was excited to decorate her space in a way that matched her older personality and style. "It was fun to try something new," she says.

2 **Keep some favorites.** Even though Hannah enjoyed getting new things for her new room, she wasn't ready to part with everything. Hannah kept her princess bookends that she's had since she was born. She also held on to the trophies and medals she earned from her former soccer, tennis, and softball leagues. "Just because everything is new doesn't mean you have to get rid of all your old stuff," Hannah says. "It made me feel better to keep some things the same."

3 **Hang out.** At first, Hannah wanted to avoid her new room because it felt so strange and different. Her mom had a different idea. She encouraged Hannah to spend more time in her room so it would start to feel more like home. Instead of playing cards with her brother in the kitchen, they played in Hannah's room. When it was time to tackle her summer reading list, she didn't sit on the living room couch. She found a cozy spot next to her bedroom window. Before long, Hannah's room started to feel more like home.

Make Your New Room Yours

Of course, it's not always possible to paint the walls or buy a new set of linens. Decorating can be expensive. Yet, there are many ways to make your room fit your style—even on a budget. Here are some low-cost and no-cost decorating tips you might try (with your parents' permission, of course!):

* Hang your favorite posters on the wall.

* Create a painting or collage.

* Re-arrange the furniture to change the space of your room.

* Paint one wall—not all of them. This can add a little color without a lot of cost.

When Your Comfort Zone Feels a Million Miles Away

Ten-year-old Tristan's favorite spot was in the living room of the house he had lived in since he was born. That's where he liked to watch television, play guitar, and play games with his friends. Tristan's mom described him as an "indoor kid" because he spent so much time hanging out in his house.

The summer before fifth grade, Tristan's parents announced that the family would be moving. They weren't just getting a new house, though. They were getting a new lifestyle. Tristan's family was moving to another state where they would live on a farm.

When Tristan first looked around his new house, he wondered whether he'd ever feel comfortable again. Not only did his parents decide there would be no television on the farm (that's right, no TV!), they told Tristan he'd be learning how to care for cows, horses, chickens, sheep, and pigs. Talk about finding a totally new comfort zone!

Luckily, Tristan packed something important when he moved. This "thing" helped him gradually find his comfort zone in a place that was completely unfamiliar. What helped this farm feel more like home? Tristan's hopeful and helpful attitude.

Optimistic

(adjective): hopeful; expecting the best in a situation.

Tristan knew this move would bring big changes, and he wasn't sure what to expect. However, he decided to be optimistic.

"I was nervous, at first," Tristan admits. "But I was kind of excited, too." Tristan had always wanted a pet pig, and now he would have one. He always loved sports, and now he'd have acres of land in his yard to run around and play ball with his brother. Tristan decided to look for things that were positive about the move. His hopeful attitude helped him feel more comfortable.

Tristan also went to his parents for help and support. When he was worried, his parents listened to his feelings. When he was looking for ways to feel more at home in his new situation, his parents offered advice. "When my parents made a suggestion, I just tried it," he says. "It was their idea for me to join the school band and get involved in a local youth group. I'm glad I did."

Tristan's parents and new neighbors also helped him learn how to take care of farm animals. Today, he feeds the animals and leads them to their pastures. He plays with his pet pig. He also spends less time in the house, and feels much more comfortable as an "outdoor kid."

Focus on the Familiar

As a new kid, you're certainly faced with plenty of changes. However, there's probably a lot in your life that's still the same. It can be comforting to notice the important things in your life that haven't changed. For example, let's say you and your family recently moved to the other side of the country where everything feels different. Even though your zip code and winter wardrobe may have changed, your family is still the same. Your mom will still be there to remind you to make the bed; your dad can still make the best banana-chocolate smoothies in the world; and your little sister will probably keep asking you to play "Go Fish" with her for the thousandth time!

Now, it's time to make a list of the things that *haven't* changed since you've become the "new kid." Here are some ideas to get you started:

* My family. They're here to help me through hard times, and to share the fun times, too.

* My stuff. I still have my sports trophies, school yearbooks, lucky sweater, and autographed poster from my favorite band.

* My sense of humor. I like to laugh a lot and that helps me feel good.

Okay, now it's your turn. Make a list of the things that are still the same about you!

Your new room may still feel like it belongs to someone else, and the kids in school may still feel like strangers. Hang in there! Before you know it, these faces and places will feel much more familiar.

Get Familiar with the Unfamiliar

It may be tough, at first, to keep track of all the new information in your life—like your bus number, address, phone number, and even the names of your new next-door neighbors. You might want to ask your parents for a small index card so you can write down the information you want to remember. Then, keep it in your backpack or wallet. That's what 11-year-old Gabriel did when he started a new middle school. "It turns out I didn't really need it much," he says, "but I was glad to have it just in case."

Check Out the Scenery

Have you ever heard of a snack called Poutine? Nine-year-old Sabrina hadn't, until her family moved from the United States to a French-speaking community in Canada. Poutine is a popular dish in Sabrina's new hometown. It's served in many fast-food restaurants and school cafeterias. What is Poutine, you ask? It is a giant plate of French fries covered with cheese curds and beef gravy. Sometimes, Poutine is served with beef spaghetti sauce on the fries instead of gravy.

In Sabrina's old neighborhood, one of her favorite comfort foods was French fries with lots and lots of ketchup. She's quite sure she never poured gravy or beef spaghetti sauce on her fries before!

However, Sabrina wasn't living in her old neighborhood anymore. Gravy-covered snacks weren't the only things that made her feel far from her comfort zone. Sabrina had spoken English throughout her life, and was now living in a community where people spoke French and English. She used to attend a small private school, and was now enrolled in a large public school. Even the weather was different (and much colder) than where she used to live.

Sabrina decided to create a new comfort zone by gathering information about her new hometown so it wouldn't feel so different. She and her parents read books about the country and its unique foods, traditions, and climate. What's more, she decided to try new things so she could feel more comfortable with all the changes.

Guess what? Sabrina tried Poutine and liked it! She even started taking French classes and is learning to ski. Even though Sabrina was a long way from her old comfort zone, she dis-

Comfort food

(noun): familiar food that reminds you of home.

covered something that felt very familiar. "I was expecting people to seem foreign and different here," she says. "But I've met people who are just like me."

One way to get more comfortable in your new zone is to explore the surroundings and check out the scenery. When Calvin and his family moved to a new state, his parents planned trips to a science museum, state park, nearby towns, the movie theater, and the bowling alley. Once, they spent the entire day at an amusement park that was located only 30 minutes from their new house. Even though Calvin wasn't in his old comfort zone, he gradually started feeling more and more comfortable in his new one.

Get Connected

You may be living in the same bedroom, but now attend a new school on the other side of town. Or, you may be living in another part of the country. Either way, you've got some new places to learn about and explore. Your parents can help you get more familiar with your new surroundings by taking you on a school tour like James's parents did, or driving you all around town like Calvin's parents did.

> My parents kept taking us to all these places in our new neighborhood so we would get used to it. Most of the time, it was pretty fun.
>
> —Calvin, 12

However, there are ways you can explore your new zone without a tour guide or a driver's license. How? Connect to the Internet. (If you don't have access to a computer at home, ask your parents to take you to the public library.) You can gather photos and information about all kinds of things you might be curious about, like: your school song, school colors, mascot, principal's name, and even whether last year's football team had a winning season. What's more, you can discover local dog-friendly restaurants, mini-golf courses, or the origin of your town's name. It might be fun to make a list of the new facts you discover and share them with your family members. You'll soon go from being a new kid to a know-it kid.

Be Flexible

Fourteen-year-old Maddie knows all about creating new comfort zones. She and her family have moved back and forth to different countries twice because of her father's job. She has lived in three different rooms, attended three different schools, and met three sets of friends in many places in the United States and throughout the world.

Maddie says there's more to creating a comfort zone than decorating your room or exploring your school or neighborhood. Being patient is an important step in feeling comfortable in your new place. When she first moved overseas, she heard some kids saying, "I can't wait to leave," as soon as they got there. Maddie says it's important to be patient and give people and places a chance. Even if you aren't excited about your new school or town, according to Maddie, you may like it better once you meet friends. "Think about it as the people you're with, not where you're living or going to school," she advises. "Once you make a great group of friends, it doesn't matter where you are."

Embrace Change

Adjusting to all kinds of changes isn't always easy. Maddie remembers feeling overwhelmed, at times, because she was dealing with a lot of new things at once. The teachers in her various schools all had different ways of teaching and the lessons were different everywhere she went. While she was busy keeping up with school work, she was also trying to meet new friends and feel more comfortable in some very unique places. "It gets kind of confusing," she says. "Setting your school life straight and finding new people to hang out with at the same time can be hard."

Stepping Out of Your Comfort Zone . . . and Into New Adventures

Remember Hannah? Her bedroom wasn't the only new thing in her life. She was living in an entirely new climate. In her old town, it never snowed. Now, Hannah's winters included ice, snow, and plenty of heavy jackets. At first, she wondered if she'd ever feel comfortable having to wear layers of clothes and dealing with cold weather. Then, a new friend and his family invited Hannah to go ice skating for the first time. After a few slightly embarrassing falls, this became one of her favorite sports. "Ice skating was something I never could have done in my old neighborhood," she says. "Now, I try to go whenever I can!"

Then, there's James. At first, nothing felt familiar in his new school. Today, he no longer feels like a new kid. In fact, he's

Big Emotions

Let's say you created a comfy reading corner in your new room. You wore your favorite worn-in basketball sneakers to your new school. You let your feelings out in a journal. You adjusted your attitude. You even spent the day with your family riding roller coasters and eating cotton candy at the local theme park. Yet, you're still not finding your new comfort zone. What's more, you may be sad, angry, or worried about all the changes in your life. Many kids experience these emotions when changes take place that seem beyond their control. This is normal. You'll likely start to feel better when you try some of the tips offered in this book. However, there may be times when your feelings are too big to handle on your own.

If you notice a difference in the way you're acting or feeling—maybe your sleeping habits have changed, your appetite has changed, or you just don't feel like yourself—it's important to share this with a trusted adult like a parent, grandparent, aunt, uncle, teacher, or school counselor. They can help get the extra support you need and deserve. You might start by saying, "I'm sad about all the changes in my life and I don't feel like myself."

You're not expected to cope with these big emotions on your own. Reach out. Help is available!

a guidance office helper who gets to show new kids around the school for the first time. He also met a new friend in school who introduced him to lacrosse, a sport he'd never played before. "I was nervous to try it because I didn't want to embarrass myself in front of people," he says. "Then I decided to change my attitude and go for it because I never would have tried lacrosse in my old neighborhood." James is glad he did. Not only did he decide that lacrosse was his favorite new sport, he joined a neighborhood team and met new friends.

Plot Summary

In this chapter, you discovered that a comfort zone isn't necessarily a place, but a feeling. You learned that you can begin to feel comfortable wherever you are with some support, patience, and a positive attitude. Last, but not least, you gathered specific ideas about how to get more comfortable when the scenes in your life have changed.

> My new school was completely different than my old one, but there were a lot of things about it that turned out to be good. At first, it felt kind of weird, but now I'm really happy there.
>
> —Gabriel, 11

Gabriel

Coming Attractions

Now that we've spent some time talking about how to get comfortable when you're not in your comfort zone, we're going to switch gears and encourage you to do exactly the opposite! We'll help you discover why it may be exciting (and even good for you) to shake things up, take new steps, and try new things. Confused? Curious? Check out Chapter Three.

CHAPTER 3

Taking New Steps

When I went to the lunch room on the first day, I was kind of worried because I didn't know who to sit with.

—David, 13

When I started my new school, the classes were pretty cool and fun. They weren't as hard as I thought they would be.

—Gianna, 11

I'll never forget the first time I walked to my new bus stop. We live in the mountains and I saw an elk standing nearby!

—Janessa, 12

As a new kid, you'll experience all kinds of "firsts." There will be a first time to walk through the double doors of your new school. There will be a first day to look for a place to sit in the lunchroom. If you move to a new house, there will also be a first night to fall asleep in an unfamiliar bedroom.

Like David, you might worry about your new situation and how to handle it. Like Gianna, some of your first experiences as a new kid may be better than you thought. Like Janessa, you may be in for a few surprises. Although, chances are, you won't see an elk near your bus stop!

It's important to remember that life is filled with new situations. It's also important to remember that new kids aren't the only ones to experience them. In fact, even if you've lived in the same room since you were born and attended the same school since kindergarten, you've probably already faced— and handled—plenty of first-time experiences.

Look Back at Changes

As a new kid, you may feel like this is the first time in your life that you've been faced with big changes. However, if you take a look back, you'll probably discover that you've successfully handled all kinds of changes even before you switched schools or moved to a new neighborhood.

Here are some examples of new situations you may have already experienced.

New Grades
Every autumn since kindergarten, you've grabbed folders, pencils, and notebook paper, and started a new grade in school. When you walked into your new classroom, you were greeted

by a new teacher and probably some kids you didn't know very well. Sure, you may have seen some familiar friends in your class. However, there's a good chance you were faced with some new faces, too.

Now, take a few minutes to think about some of the friends you've met each school year. Do you remember how you met them? What did you talk about? What made you interested in getting to know them? How long did it take until you felt like you became good friends?

Sports Teams

Did your love of hoops inspire you to join a basketball league? Were you kicking balls in the living room before you decided to sign up for a soccer team? Sure, you may have joined a new team with a friend or two. However, you probably didn't know everyone on the team when you started. You had to meet new coaches, get to know new kids, and learn new rules.
What were your first impressions of the coaches and the players? Did they change over time, or stay the same? How did you get to know your fellow teammates? How did you figure out the coaches' unique teaching styles and what they were looking for in the players?

Clubs and Summer Programs

Have you ever made a lanyard at day camp? Have you slept under the stars at a sleep-away camp? Have you been part of a scouting program, robotics team, service club, or chorus? Any group activity includes some new faces and places. Even if you signed up with your best friend, you probably met some new friends, got to know new teachers and counselors, and participated in new activities you hadn't experienced before.

What made you interested in one activity over another? How much time did you give yourself to see if you really liked it? What did you do to get to know kids in your group? How did you let others know you were interested in getting to know them? What did you want the counselors and other kids to know about you?

These examples may not seem as dramatic as starting a new school or moving across the country, but these were times when you had to walk into a new situation and take some new steps. See? You've already practiced some helpful skills and probably didn't even realize it!

Your Steps, Your Style

Your parents and other trusted adults can help you handle new situations by offering great advice and support. However, they can't take new steps for you. As much as your parents would probably love to follow you around on the first day of school to help you find your classrooms or introduce you to a nice guy or girl to sit with in the lunchroom—they can't. Besides, we're pretty sure that's not something you'd want anyway! Remember, you've already taken plenty of new steps in your life—long before you switched schools or moved to a new town. Now, let's explore your taking-new-steps style.

> It's normal to be nervous about change, but usually things turn out fine.
>
> **—Aaron, 10**

What's Your New-Steps Style?

Rate yourself on each of the following statements from 1 (definitely do not agree) to 5 (strongly agree).

_____ I don't enjoy trying new foods. I'm fine sticking with the tastes I already know.

_____ Even though I've been curious about styling my hair differently, I wouldn't feel comfortable changing my look.

_____ I just finished reading the entire book series by my favorite author, and it was awesome! I don't want to start a new series by someone else because it probably won't be as good.

_____ I've been invited to my cousin's bowling birthday party, but I don't know any of her friends. I love my cousin and I like to bowl, but I'd rather stay home than have to say hi to people I don't know.

_____ My drama teacher just announced her retirement. She taught me everything I know, and I doubt I'll learn as much from a new teacher.

_____ My older brother wants to teach me how to play tennis so we can play together. I'm not sure I'll be good at it, so I ask him to play with someone else.

_____ **Total**

About your score:

20–30: You might tend to feel uneasy about taking new steps and probably avoid making too many changes in your life. It's normal to want things to stay the same. However, everyone is faced with taking new steps at one time or another. Keep reading and make a plan so you can learn some ways to cope with change and take those steps with confidence and optimism.

6–20: Even though you recognize that new steps can be scary sometimes, you believe that change might bring interesting new experiences and people into your life.

It can be kind of boring when everything stays exactly the same.

—Hannah, 14

Step Out of Your Zone

It's certainly nice to feel comfortable and recognize the faces and places in your life. However, as you read at the end of the last chapter, there may be some advantages to stepping outside your comfort zone. You might discover a new hobby or meet new friends. When you face a new situation, you also face new opportunities—and maybe even some exciting new adventures. You have already taken lots of new steps. Now you need to take another and be ready to step out of your comfort zone.

Thirteen-year-old David stepped out of his very comfortable zone. He had attended a small private school since kindergarten, and knew every kid and every teacher in the building. During fifth grade, David's parents approached him about starting sixth grade at the local public school. They wanted David to meet kids from the neighborhood and have the opportunity to participate on some of the many sports teams offered at the larger school. David was nervous, but decided he was ready for a change. He stepped out of his comfort zone and into a new school. There, he made many new friends—including some who live on a nearby street. He keeps up with old friends, as well. David is also a starting player on the school basketball team. With his parents' encouragement and support, David stepped out of his comfort zone and is glad he did.

You get to experience so many new things when you move or switch schools. You're not kept in this little box of what it's like to only be in one place.

—Maddie, 14

My mom wanted me to do an after school activity that I didn't really want to do. It was an improv group. I really didn't want to go, but I went anyway. That's where I ended up meeting my best friend.

—Luke, 9

We moved because my dad got a new job. In his old job, he had to be away a lot on the weekends. Now he's home more. I'm happy the whole family is together now.

—Sabrina, 9

Sabrina

Prepare for Setbacks

As you get ready to take new steps, know that you might encounter setbacks or challenging situations. There's a difference between worrying about potential challenges and preparing for them. While you shouldn't expect things to go poorly, you might be more confident about taking new steps if you know that you have a plan to deal with tough spots.

Abigail is a taking-new-steps expert. Her father is in the U.S. military, and his job takes the family all over the world. In fact, moving has been part of Abigail's life for as long as she can remember. Most recently, her family moved from the United States to Japan. "I was sad to say goodbye to my friends," Abigail says. "We lived in the last place for almost three years and that was a long time for us." Not only was Abigail leaving good friends behind, she was moving to a new country with an entirely different language, different food, and different way of life. That's a lot of new steps at once.

Abigail was 12 when she and her family moved to Japan. She was enrolled in a school for military families, so most of the kids spoke English. That helped her feel a little less nervous as she took those new steps into her classroom. However, Abigail's first few days weren't easy. "Some of the kids in my new class weren't nice to me; they teased me and bullied me," she says. "It didn't go well." Abigail felt worried and upset. She'd moved many times before and hadn't experienced this type of behavior from others. In fact, Abigail recalls that the majority of the kids she's met over the years have been welcoming, kind, and eager to meet her.

Abigail remembered learning about bullying during an assembly at her previous school. She and her friends had watched a play about how to handle tough situations like bullying. At first, Abigail chose to ignore the kids who were

Bullies

Most of the time, kids are friendly and want to get to know new guys and girls. Abigail says she met many nice friends each time she moved. However, teasing and bullying can happen anywhere, whether you're a new kid or not.

People will bully others for all kinds of reasons. Bullies may be insecure. They may be looking for a way to feel powerful and in control of their lives. They may even be bullied at home by a parent or other family member, and are repeating this behavior with others. Regardless of the reason, treating people badly—through hurtful words or actions—is never okay. If you're being bullied, it's important to remember that it's not your fault, you're not alone, and help is available.

If you feel uncomfortable or unsafe in your school, talk with a parent or school counselor to find the best way to handle the situation. It takes courage to reach out and ask for help. Abigail reached out to her parents, and she's glad she did.

teasing her. When their behavior continued, she felt sad and worried. Abigail remembered learning that if you feel frightened by another person, it's important to tell an adult. She decided to tell her parents what was happening. They listened to her concerns and contacted the school.

Abigail's parents and teacher worked together to address the situation and help figure out the best strategies. The school counselor met with Abigail privately to talk about ways she could respond to the kids who were teasing her. The counselor also met with the other kids—as well as their parents—to address the hurtful behaviors. The counselor introduced Abigail to some new guys and girls at her school. She joined an after-school club and started to develop new friendships.

Things did change for the better. One of the kids Abigail met was a girl with the same first name, and they discovered they shared other things in common, too. "We became good friends," she says. "That's when things started to work out."

Boost Your Confidence

Although taking new steps can be scary at first, they can bring plenty of rewards, like new friends, new lessons, and even new confidence. Take a look at some potentially first-rate new situations and their benefits:

* **New step:** Moving into your new home.

* **What you may gain:** A more flexible personality and the ability to adjust to new surroundings.

* **New step:** Starting a new school.

* **What you may gain:** New opportunities to learn and meet new people.

* **New step:** Introducing yourself to kids you'd like to meet.

* **What you may gain:** A sense of confidence and courage, and, before you know it, some really great friends.

As you can see, taking new steps can be beneficial. They can also be fun. Here are a few you might enjoy:

* **New Activities:** Auditioning for a part in the school play even if you've never acted before.

* **New Look:** Choosing a completely new hairstyle for your school picture.

* **New Skills:** Signing up for a French class despite the fact that you can't pronounce *bonjour*.

* **New Friends:** Asking your biology lab partner to the school dance, even if you're not sure what the answer will be.

* **New Foods:** Tasting tofu "meat" loaf because you can't believe that it's actually food!

Know Which Steps to Avoid

Not all new steps are necessarily good ones. Make sure the steps you take will help you learn, grow, and enhance your life. Just for fun, we're going to list a few to **avoid**:

* Don't ride your new bike off a ten-foot dirt ramp on a dare

* Don't take the math test after watching an all-night marathon of your favorite television show

* Don't paint your dog's toenails red…while sitting on the white carpet in your parents' bedroom

* Avoid any new experience that may be hazardous to your health or well-being or the health and well-being of others—or that might require the use of a stunt double

Some kids might think that accepting a dare will help them fit in with a new crowd. This is never a good idea. It takes courage to say no to something that doesn't feel right, especially when you're just getting to know new people. However, if you're feeling pressured to accept a dare in order to fit in with a new group, it's important to ask yourself, "Would a true friend put me in an uncomfortable situation or pressure me to do something I don't want to do?" When you stay true to your beliefs, you'll stay on the path to finding the friends who respect you, accept you, and share your values.

Ready, Set, Take Those Steps

There are many positive ways to try new things and step out of your comfort zone. We have talked about a few. Here are some more tips to help you get started taking new steps.

* **Plan ahead.** Talk to your parents and let them know you're thinking about trying something new. You might say, "Now that I'm in a new school (or a new town), I'm curious about what I can do here that I haven't experienced before— maybe a new sport, activity, or club. Can you help me find out what's available?"

* **Start slowly.** Even if you're feeling especially adventurous, you might want to take new steps slowly, rather than all at once. For example, you're probably eager to meet a new group of friends. However, you might feel more comfortable introducing yourself to one or two new faces at a time, rather than walking up to an entire table of kids in the lunch room and saying hello.

* **Hold on to the familiar.** Taking new steps doesn't mean changing your entire life. In fact, you've probably experienced plenty of changes and may not be interested in adding too many more! Even if you're interested in meeting new friends or trying a new sport, hold on to valued friendships and interests. It may be helpful to view new steps as a way to add positive experiences to your life, not to forget about your past experiences.

* **Be patient and realistic.** Trying a new sport or joining a new club may not feel exciting, at first. It may just feel scary or uncomfortable. You might want to give yourself a little time before deciding whether it's for you. However, don't feel pressured to take on all kinds of new experiences at once. If you're not enjoying a new club or hobby, it's okay to try something else or simply take a break for now.

* **Ask for help.** If you're having trouble finding positive ways to take new steps and enjoy your new experiences, talk to a parent or other trusted adult. Reaching out to others and sharing your feelings are important ways to adjust to the changes in your life.

* **Believe in yourself.** Sometimes, people have to take new steps—like Calvin and Janessa did when their families moved. Other times, people intentionally seek new steps because they're eager to experience new things. That's what David did when he and his parents decided he should attend a large public school after spending six years at a small private school. Either way, it's important to believe in yourself and your ability to make the most of your new situation. It may not be easy, at first. An optimistic outlook can help. In time—and with support—things get better.

Plot Summary

Chapter Three is all about taking new steps in life, just like you're doing right now. In fact, you've already taken many new steps in your life, and maybe didn't realize it! Even before you were a new kid, you started new grades in school and possibly joined a new team or went to a camp without many close friends. In this chapter, you learned that you've already developed many skills for taking new steps. You also learned that taking new steps can build confidence and even bring new opportunities.

 Coming Attractions

Before you jump into your new steps, you'll probably experience some in-between time. What's that? Read on to learn what it is, and how to make the most of it!

CHAPTER 4

Playing the Waiting Game

> Because I didn't know anybody yet, my brother and I went to the golf course a few times a week.
>
> —Calvin, 12

> We moved during winter break, so I didn't meet anyone right away. I hung out with my sisters and we played board games. I also spent a lot of time unpacking and putting my stuff where I wanted it.
>
> —James, 13

> I didn't do much of anything. I just waited.
>
> —David, 13

efore you became a new kid, you probably had plenty of ways to keep busy. Chances are, many of these ways involved making plans with friends. A movie night, weekly soccer practice, or sleepovers—your friends were likely as close as a quick phone call or text message. Now, it may seem as if someone has pushed the "pause" button on your life.

Your old friends may no longer be nearby, and you haven't met new ones yet. You still want to see the new action movie, play on a sports team, and stay up late talking with friends. Yet, you don't have any names to call on your speed dial. You're probably feeling like you're living in the middle of two different lives.

Welcome to your in-between time! This period usually doesn't last long, but it's important to make the most of it.

What to Do

There's more than one way to fill your in-between time. You might enjoy filling your days with all kinds of activities. You may prefer having some quiet time—especially if you're usually very busy. Or you might be okay spending lots of time on your own. Any of these choices is fine. The key is to look for fun and positive activities that you'll enjoy while waiting to feel more settled in your new situation. First, think about what you like to do and figure out how you like to wait.

In-between time

(noun): the days or weeks you spend waiting to meet new friends and make new plans after experiencing a change or transition in your life.

CASTING CALL

Which Way Do You Wait?

Here's a quiz to help you discover your unique waiting style, and help you figure out the best way to spend your in-between time.

1. **Your family is taking a four-hour car ride to visit your grandparents. It feels like you've been on the road for hours, but it's only been 25 minutes. What do you do?**
   a) Play cards with your mom and choose a new type of card game each time you pass 100 miles.
   b) Enjoy chatting with your family, but not every minute. After all, there are only so many hours you can listen to your brother talk about his sports trading card collection.
   c) Listen to music on your MP3 player, and even take a nap for a little while. You'll get there before you know it.

2. **It's time for your yearly physical, and your doctor is running behind. You're sitting in a waiting room with your dad, a bunch of baby toys, a pile of magazines, and a television that's stuck on the cartoon channel. What do you do?**
   a) Call your best friend and talk about what's been happening at school.
   b) Read a magazine and bring your dad up to date on all the celebrity gossip.
   c) Do a crossword puzzle without any help. That's a sure way to keep you occupied.

3. **Tomorrow morning, your drama teacher will post the names of the students who are getting a role in the school play. You have to wait 16 more hours to find out if you got the lead. What do you do?**
   a) Spend every minute with your friends to keep your mind distracted. You even convince your parents to let you have a sleepover on a school night.

b) Spend a little time researching the play online so you can be prepared if you're called for a role. Play some basketball with your neighbors. Then, hang out in your room and get ready for bed—because every actor needs a good night's sleep.

c) Read a book and do your homework. Tomorrow will be here soon enough.

About your score:

Mostly A's: You probably want your daily calendar to be filled from top to bottom. You're happiest when you have something to do and someone to do it with. As a new kid, it may be tough to wait for your schedule to fill up again. In your in-between time, you'll probably want to look for activities that involve other people—even if that means you'll be hanging out with your family for the next few days or weeks! Keep some of your days free, though. This may be a good opportunity to learn how to enjoy your own company for a change. Even though you're a full-time "people person," don't overlook the joys of spending time with one of the most important people of all: You!

Mostly B's: You may enjoy being busy with others, but you're also okay spending time on your own. During your in-between time, look for activities that keep you connected with people (yes, even your little sister). However, be sure to schedule some alone time so you can develop new interests, read a favorite book, or just relax for a while. Before you know it, you'll be filling up that social calendar again.

Mostly C's: You're an expert at entertaining yourself without the need for a crowd. You don't need much to keep you busy. A challenging puzzle or a favorite playlist is often enough to help you pass the time with ease. It's great that you can enjoy your own company, but don't pass up opportunities to spend some of your in-between time with others. Your parents and siblings can be great company (and also great support) as you gradually get more comfortable with your new situation.

Find a Crowd

There are other ways kids have kept busy during their in-between time. Some of these ideas may be right for you. Look for activities that fit your unique style and interests. Then, go ahead and make a list with a few ideas of your own. If you constantly crave a crowd, you might want to try these ideas:

* **Play ball.** Challenge your little sister to a game of basketball. While you're outside, you might even meet a new neighbor or two.

* **Hang with your family.** Play cards, watch a video, or take a long walk together. You may even discover that your little brother's not that annoying, after all!

* **Cook a meal.** If chocolate and banana pancakes are your favorite breakfast, why wait for a special occasion to make them? Ask a parent to teach you how to cook your favorite meals, and try out some new recipes for your family while you're at it.

* **Make a difference.** Ask your parents to help you find a community agency that welcomes volunteers of all ages. You might work in an animal shelter, participate in a beach cleanup, or enter a walk-a-thon to benefit a charitable organization. Not only will you be helping people, you'll be around others who care about the same things you do.

* **Plan a family outing.** Whether you're new in town, or you've lived there your whole life, there is always some-thing new to discover wherever you are. Ask each member of your family what activities they enjoy the most and plan a fun afternoon together.

* **Call your grandma, your cousin, or your favorite uncle.** If you have relatives nearby, now would be a great time to visit. If your relatives live far away, pick up the phone to call and catch up. There's probably a funny story about one of your family members that you haven't heard yet.

Try New Activities

If you seek a balance between hanging out with others and hanging out on your own, these activities might be up your alley:

* **Speak a new language.** Thinking about a future career as a translator in a far-away country? Planning an around-the-world trip one day? Ask your parents to take you to the library or look online together to learn some key words and phrases in a few different languages. You never know when these will come in handy!

* **Deck the walls.** Cut out pictures from magazines to decorate your new room or your locker at school. That'll make your space feel more personal. While you're at it, invite your little brother or sister to help. It might be a fun way to bond while you're waiting to meet new friends.

* **Plan your birthday party.** You may not have many names on your guest list yet, but that shouldn't get in the way of your plans. Before you know it, you'll meet plenty of kids to celebrate your big day. Besides, it's never too soon to plan a party!

* **Check in.** Keeping in touch with old friends can be a great way to pass the time and stay connected. Go ahead and call or text to say hello. Just be careful not to spend too much time chatting with old friends. It's important to give yourself plenty of opportunities to meet new ones, as well.

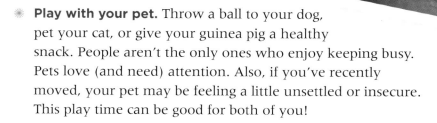

> My parents drove us around the neighborhood a lot so we could get to know places. We hiked. We went to the rodeo. I hung out a lot with my brother and sister.
>
> **—Janessa, 12**

* **Play with your pet.** Throw a ball to your dog, pet your cat, or give your guinea pig a healthy snack. People aren't the only ones who enjoy keeping busy. Pets love (and need) attention. Also, if you've recently moved, your pet may be feeling a little unsettled or insecure. This play time can be good for both of you!

* **Help your parents unpack.** Okay, so this may not be the most exciting way to spend your in-between time. However, it's a nice thing to do and your parents will appreciate it. What's more, it'll help you. How else are you going to find a spoon when you're eating your favorite breakfast cereal?

Entertain Yourself

If you can entertain yourself with ease, try these ideas:

* **Get the facts.** Go online to learn some fun facts about your new town or school. Soon, you'll feel like an expert in your new place.

* **Document your life.** Start a scrapbook to record your new adventures. It'll be fun to look back and see all the new experiences you've had.

* **Learn the words.** There's no time like the present to learn your new school song. When you're at your first pep rally or football game, you can sing loud and proud.

* **Try a new talent.** Have you always wanted to paint? Play an instrument? Dribble a basketball with both hands? Right now you've got plenty of time to practice. Enjoy it.

* **Explore the world—from home.** Do you know what the Great Wall of China looks like? Have you seen the Mona Lisa in the Louvre? You can see the world without ever leaving your neighborhood by taking a virtual tour of the places you've always wanted to visit. You'll need some free time (you've got that!); a computer with an Internet connection (your local library has computers if you don't have one available at home); and an adventurous spirit. Bon Voyage.

* **Boost your brain.** One of the best ways to keep busy and improve your brain power at the same time is to do a crossword puzzle, brainteaser, or math game. If you really want to challenge yourself, try doing the puzzles with a pen. No erasing!

Even if you're okay just relaxing and doing nothing once in a while, it can be helpful to keep a list of fun activities handy in case you're ready for a change of pace. Grab some paper or open a new file on your computer and make a list of your own.

What's My Next Line?

Loneliness

Even if you're really good at keeping busy during your in-between time, there's still a good chance you miss your old friends and wish you had them nearby to enjoy the things you used to do together. That's understandable. It's hard to be away from people you care about. You may be sad or lonely. It can be difficult to handle these big emotions, especially when you're facing so many changes in your life. It's important for you to know that you're not expected to handle all of these emotions or changes alone. Share what's on your mind with a parent or another adult you trust (like a grandparent, aunt, or uncle). Reaching out to the adults in your life is an important step towards feeling better.

Plot Summary

In this chapter, you learned about in-between time: the days
or weeks you spend waiting to meet new friends and make
new plans after experiencing a change or transition in your life.
You also discovered there are many ways to spend this time
and enjoy your own company (and maybe even your little
brother's).

 Coming Attractions

Even though you've learned all kinds of ways to keep busy
during your in-between time, you'll soon be spending more
time with others and meeting new friends. Read all about
it in Chapter 5.

CHAPTER 5

Making New Friends

n the spring of their fifth and sixth grades, sisters Angie and Gianna were looking forward to summer camp and end-of-the year graduation parties. They were also looking forward to another year of school with the friends they'd known since kindergarten. However, Angie and Gianna's parents had other plans.

"One day, our mom and dad told us we were going to a private school that we'd never heard of," explains Angie. "My sister and I didn't want to go because we wanted to go to school with our friends. We put up this whole fight." Eventually, Angie and Gianna agreed to visit the school and take a tour. It turns out, they liked it. But even though they liked their new school, they spent the rest of the summer stressing about starting over.

It can be stressful to start over and meet new friends, especially when you've known the same people for so long. "I always had friends around," Gianna says. "With half of them, I didn't even remember how we became friends. We just grew up together, so they were always there."

Remember Your First Friendships

When you were very young, you didn't have to think too much about how to meet friends. Take a moment to remember some of your first friends. One might have been the boy who built tall towers with you in preschool. Another may have been the girl who shared the swing on the playground with you. The point is, early friendships usually develop quickly and easily. However, they also change frequently and don't involve finding someone to share your interests or spill personal details about your life. Most likely, your earliest friendships developed because you wanted someone to play with.

Now, hit the "fast forward" button to today. It's great to introduce yourself to kids you've never met, but at your age you're probably not going to do it by asking if they want to play with you. (At least, we wouldn't recommend it!)

These days, you're looking for relationships with guys and girls who share your interests, values, and maybe even your sense of humor. You're looking for friends you can talk to, feel comfortable around, trust, and share fun experiences with. These relationships may take time to develop.

Take a Look at You

Before you begin looking around for new people to call "friends," it's important to spend some time getting to know one of the most important people in your life: You!

As you grow, you're not only changing on the outside. You're likely changing on the inside, as well. Maybe you used to listen to Top 40 music. However, since you started guitar lessons, you're all about rock these days. Perhaps your idea of a fun weekend morning used to be playing video games in your living room, but now you'd rather challenge someone to a full-court basketball game at the local community center. When you were younger, your neighbor's dog, Fluffy, used to scare you. Today, you may be an avid animal lover.

Because many of your interests, values, and priorities may be different today than they were a few years ago, it can be worthwhile (and even fun!) to think about what's interesting and important to you these days. Not only will this help you get to know yourself a little better, it can help you decide what you might be looking for in a friend. It can also be a great way to narrow down the best places to meet new friends, but we'll get to that a little later. Stay tuned!

Just for fun, imagine you're a celebrity who's about to be featured in an entertainment magazine. Before the interview, your manager tells you that you're going to be asked all kinds of questions about yourself to let fans get to know you better. Then, he hands you a sheet of paper and says, "Write down the three most important things you'd like other people to know about you to help the journalist tell your story."

Now, go ahead and grab a blank piece of paper or open a new document on your computer and start writing! Here are some ideas to help you get started:

* How do you like to spend your free time? For example, do you have a favorite sport or hobby?

* What are you watching, reading, and listening to? Name your favorite movies, television shows, books, and musicians.

* What matters to you? Are you passionate about politics? Do you recycle everything from bottles to batteries? Maybe you're a frequent volunteer at the animal shelter? Take a moment to list the causes and issues you care most about.

Keep an Open Mind

Because your personality is actually a wonderful mix of moods, interests, and behaviors, you're not just one "type" of person. You're remarkable. You're unique. You're constantly growing and changing.

Guess what? The same can be said for many of the guys and girls you'll be meeting. Chances are, they can't be described in just a few words either. Instead of judging people based on a handful of first impressions or behaviors, you might want to give them a chance and get to know them.

That's what Angie and Gianna did.

On the first day of school, Gianna decided to try and meet as many people as she could without making quick decisions about them. "I wanted to get to know people," she explains. "I wanted to keep my eyes open, be open-minded, and not look for a specific type of person."

Her sister, Angie, also resisted the urge to judge people based on first impressions. "You're not supposed to judge a book by its cover, but it's easy to do," she admits. Like Gianna, Angie decided to keep an open mind and be friendly to others. She remembers wondering whether each person she met would

I was nervous because I didn't know what kind of people I would meet. I had all these ideas about what people would be like, and I was wrong. It made me feel better that most of them were just like me.

—Gianna, 11

Who Am I . . . Today?

If you were asked to describe yourself in three words, which words would you choose? Here's a list of common adjectives. Just for fun, circle the top three words that best describe your personality. Remember, you can only choose three:

funny	kind	caring	generous
silly	talkative	serious	cautious
adventurous	honest	sarcastic	quiet
outgoing	athletic	inquisitive	studious
patient	polite	creative	logical
friendly	flexible	optimistic	independent
shy	social	loud	playful
apprehensive	enthusiastic	trustworthy	loyal
outspoken	thoughtful	confident	talented
pensive	spiritual	ambitious	dramatic

Now, go back to the list and circle three additional words that describe you. Did it? Great! Now, look at the list one more time and circle three more.

Even after having circled all those words, are you able to find adjectives to describe yourself? You probably can. That's because there's a good chance you'll identify with all of these personality traits at one time or another. In fact, you might feel friendly, creative, independent, athletic, loyal, and apprehensive—all in the same day!

turn out to be nice or not-so-nice. "I wanted to let it be a surprise!" she says.

Meet Your Match

As a new kid, you'll be meeting guys and girls with a variety of interests, values, personalities and backgrounds. However, you won't necessarily become close friends with all of them. That's okay. Many kids say they prefer having a few trusted friends over having a lot of casual acquaintances.

There's no mathematical formula for making friends. Sometimes, you might be interested in getting to know someone because you share similar interests. Other times, you might want to become someone's friend because you don't share similar interests but you're eager to learn new things.

There's also no rule that says your friends should be exactly like you. In fact, as you read in Chapter 3, it can be fun to expand your horizons.

However, it can be helpful to think about some of the general qualities you value in a friend to help narrow your search and increase the likelihood of meeting people whose company you'll enjoy.

Acquaintance

(noun): someone you know, but not a close friend.

Expanding horizons

(verb): seeking new friendships, new hobbies, or new experiences that may enhance your life.

Watch and Wait

Some kids prefer to take their time and get to know people before trying to make friends. Now that you've identified what you look for in a friend, you might want to spend your first few days in your new school paying attention and learning about your classmates.

CASTING CALL **What Do You Look for in a Friend?**

Think about a really close friend you've had in your life. Now, list five things about him or her that you appreciated. What were some qualities you admired? Why were you interested in getting to know this person? What was it about this friend that made you know you could spill your secret crush without fear that this information would be shared with your entire gym class?

1.

2.

3.

4.

5.

Take a look at your responses. Did you list qualities like, "Wore the coolest clothes," or, "Was president of the class"? Probably not. Even if your best friend did own some awesome sneakers or held an important job on the student council, those probably weren't the reasons you became close friends. More likely, you were interested in the person, not his or her wardrobe or elected position.

In fact, you're not alone. SmartGirl.org asked more than 1,200 girls and boys to list the personality traits they value most in a best friend. The top three responses were: loyal, caring, and a good listener. What didn't matter much? Money, popularity, or looks.

It's likely that you already have many of the qualities that make a good friend. That'll make it easier for friends to find you. You also know what qualities you value in others. That'll make it easier to find new people to meet. After all, it helps when you know what you're looking for!

Pilar was in the third grade when she switched from a small private school with only 10 kids in her class to a large public school with more than 25 kids in every classroom. She was nervous, at first. She wondered how she would meet friends in a big school. Pilar's teacher helped ease her worries. She introduced Pilar to the guys and girls in her class, and then asked everyone to play a game called "The Friend Scavenger Hunt." This is a game where kids get to know other kids by asking questions about their interests. For example, they might be asked to find someone who plays baseball, loves broccoli, or can speak another language. This game was a fun way for kids to approach each other and get to know one another. "That's how I learned everyone's name and they learned mine," Pilar recalls.

Learning people's names was one thing. Getting to know the people under the names was another. Pilar decided she wanted to take her time. Even though she was eager to meet new people, Pilar said she didn't want to rush into friendships. She wanted to know more about them.

Pilar decided to pay attention to how the kids in her new school treated others. "I noticed people in the playground and at lunch and watched to see if they were being nice to others," she says. "When I saw how they were treating people, it helped me know if they might be a good friend."

Nine-year-old Margaret had the same idea. When her parents told her she was switching to a new school, she wondered, "How will I make new friends?" Margaret spent the first few days at her new school paying attention to how her classmates treated other people. "If they were talking to other people and acting nice, then I said hello to them," she explains. "If they smiled at me, I smiled back. Also, if they asked me my name, I thought they were probably nice and I tried to get to know them."

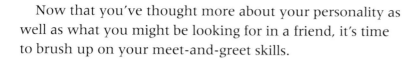

> I started talking to different people. I decided to hang out a few times to get to know them. I asked myself, 'Is this person mean? Is this one nice?' That helped me decide who to be friends with.
>
> **—David, 13**

Now that you've thought more about your personality as well as what you might be looking for in a friend, it's time to brush up on your meet-and-greet skills.

Meet and Greet

It's hard to pin down an exact number, but one study suggests that guys and girls will make an average of 406 friends in a lifetime. That means you'll have plenty of opportunities to practice your meet-and-greet skills as you grow!

Introducing yourself to others doesn't require special training. What's more, it doesn't have to be uncomfortable or scary. The first step is to find a friendly face—in class, on your sports team, or on the school bus—and consider opening the door to a conversation. Here are a few quick and easy meet-and-greet lines you can try out, or use for inspiration to create some of your own.

✳ At the bus stop: "This is the middle school bus, right? I'd hate to get on the wrong bus on my first day here!"

✳ In class: "Do you like that book you're reading? It looks good!"

✳ At lunch: "I think I'll pass on the mystery meat today. Do you know what you're getting? What's good?"

"I met this one girl just because I was sitting next to her. She was really nice and she introduced me to everyone in the class and at the lunch table. That's how I met even more friends.

—Maddie, 14

"My teachers were really nice. They assigned group projects and had everyone work together on things to help us get to know each other."

—Yasmin, 11

"When you make one friend, he's probably friends with at least one other person. That person is probably friends with at least one other person. So even if you only meet one friend, you might have sixteen friends by the end of the day!"

—Calvin, 12

Calvin

* At practice: "Hey, I'm new in town. Can you tell me the best place to buy cleats?"

There may be times when it just feels too scary to walk up to someone new and say hello. Even thinking about it might make your cheeks flush, your heart race, or your skin feel clammy. Starting conversations with people you don't know can seem overwhelming for many kids (and plenty of adults, too!). If you're not comfortable starting a conversation right away, that's okay. You can meet people at your own pace.

The key is to take small steps forward. For example, you might want to spend a little time observing different kids in school and noticing guys and girls who seem to have interests that you share. You might notice that the girl sitting next to you in English class has a keychain on her backpack with the logo of your favorite basketball team. Or the guy on your bus is reading the same book that you're reading. These similarities can lead to easier conversation-starters than just introducing yourself to say hi. You might smile and say, "I'm a fan of that team, too. Who's your favorite player?" Or, "I'm reading that book, too. How do you like it?" If you're not quite ready to launch a conversation yet, you might want to smile or make eye-contact to show your interest. These gestures might lead to a friendly smile back, and maybe even an introduction.

If you're still uncomfortable or worried about meeting others, share your concerns with your parents or a counselor so they can help you feel more at ease.

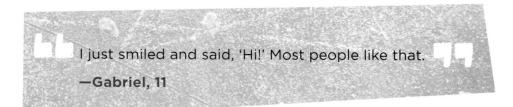

I just smiled and said, 'Hi!' Most people like that.

—Gabriel, 11

Get Out There

If you're ready to find some guys and girls to meet and greet, here are some ideas to help you get started:

* Sign-up for an after-school activity—anything from the academic bowl to the yearbook.

* Introduce yourself to at least one person in each of your classes. You might start with something like, "Hi, I'm Kendra and I'm new here."

* If you see a kickball game going on outside your house, ask if you can join in. This can be a great way to meet the neighbors (with your parents' permission, of course).

* Join a youth group through your church, temple, or other faith-based organization.

* Sign up for a neighborhood sports league.

* Volunteer!

* Try out for the school play.

* If you moved to a new town, your parents will be meeting new friends, too. Remind them to keep their eyes open for people with kids your age.

* Sign up for a class or activity you've never tried before, but have always been interested in, like cooking or chess.

* Talk to your school counselor. He or she may have some ideas to help you meet new friends in school. Many schools have "buddy" programs and other ways to help new kids feel more comfortable.

When Things Aren't Clicking

What if you keep an open mind, look for kids who might share your values (and possibly even your interest in basketball trading cards), and offer your best meet-and-greet lines, yet the conversation doesn't flow? Or, maybe the person doesn't seem overly interested in becoming your friend?

There are all kinds of reasons why some people click and others don't.

There are also all kinds of reasons why some people might not be very talkative. These reasons may have absolutely nothing to do with you.

Click

(verb): to fit together; function well together.

Maybe the girl you approached at the bus stop just found out she has to re-write her English paper because she accidentally turned in a report on the wrong book. Or the guy you said hi to in the lunchroom actually ate the mystery meat and isn't feeling too well.

When a conversation isn't flowing, don't push it. Be patient and keep a positive attitude. That's what James did. He says, "If you try to make a friend and don't succeed, just wait. Eventually, someone will come to you and try to be your friend."

If you still feel worried about making new friends, you're having trouble getting to know people, or you're feeling shy or uncomfortable about trying to meet new friends, talk to an adult you trust, like a parent, step-parent, or grandparent. Your school counselor can also offer help and advice.

Keep Your Options Open

Once you become friendly with a new guy or girl, you may be so happy to start spending time together and getting to know each other that you might accidentally ignore other people who are trying to meet you, too. It may be challenging to find the time to get to know your new friend, while still remaining open to meeting other new friends. It can be a tricky balancing act! If you're enjoying your new friend, keep making plans so you can get to know each other better. But keep your eyes open for other potential friends, as well. When you remain open to meeting a variety of guys and girls, you'll likely discover all kinds of new and interesting people in your life.

 ## Plot Summary

In this chapter, you learned the importance of getting to know yourself so you can meet friends who share your values. You also learned the benefits of keeping an open mind when meeting new guys and girls. It can be fun getting to know people with a variety of interests and ideas.

 ## Coming Attractions

Finding your place in a new group of friends can be great, but it's not always easy. Learn how to fit in with—without barging in on—established friendships. Read on.

> "I'm not going to become friends with everyone I meet, but I'm okay with that."
>
> —Aaron, 10

CHAPTER 6

Fitting in Without Barging in or Becoming Someone You're Not

> It was strange starting a new school in the middle of the year. I felt like everyone knew each other and I was an outsider.
>
> **—Malik, 12**

> The kids in my school talked about things that I didn't know about, like places they went together and things they did. I understood why it was happening, but I still felt left out.
>
> **—Nick, 10**

> I met my friend Lainie the first week of school, but she already had a best friend. I was worried that I would tear them apart.
>
> **—Janessa, 12**

**W**hen you're a new kid, there's a good chance you'll be meeting guys and girls who've known one another for a long time. They may have had years of inside jokes, sleepovers, and even family vacations together. Like Malik, Nick, and Janessa, you may be eager to make new friends, but also worried about getting in the way of other people's relationships. In other words, you want to fit in without barging in.

You may be fitting in if:

✳ you get to know a few kids in your history class and casually ask if anyone wants to catch a movie with you this weekend.

✳ your softball teammates seem nice, so you invite them to your house for pizza after the practice (with your parents' permission, of course!).

✳ you understand that the guys and girls you meet have other friends besides you—and you're okay with that.

Fitting in

(verb): gradually developing friendships with others, feeling comfortable around them, and enjoying shared experiences.

Barging in

(verb): rushing into relationships too soon, or expecting others to avoid their old friends in order to spend more time with you.

* you take time getting to know someone because friendships can't be rushed.

You may be barging in if:

* you expect an invitation to the birthday party of the girl who sits next to you in math class, but you don't even know her last name yet.

* you want your new friends to stop spending so much time with their old ones because you're the one who needs someone to hang out with at the mall.

* you refer to a new acquaintance as "My BFF." (Some of the kids you meet may turn out to be your Best Friend Forever, but it may be way too soon for that term!).

Be Yourself

Fitting in doesn't just mean that you're not barging in on other people. It also means that you're not pushing yourself into being someone you're not. The best way to fit in is to find friends who appreciate the real you.

Fourteen-year-old Grace switched from a small private school, with only forty kids in her grade, to one of the biggest schools in the United States. She was eager to meet new friends and decided she wanted to be in a "popular" clique.

"At the beginning of school, I noticed this group of girls who always hung out together and seemed popular," Grace says. "I wanted to try to be like them so I could fit in." After spending a few weeks with these girls, however, Grace had some concerns. "They had a nickname for their group, which I thought was a little weird," she says. "They also seemed kind of mean." Although Grace was eager to meet friends, she began to question whether these were the right ones for her.

One day, Grace was sitting at lunch with her new group of friends when a cute guy walked by and sat at the table next to them. All of a sudden, her new friends got up and moved to the other table to sit with him, leaving Grace behind. Only one of the girls stayed with her. "That's when I decided this group wasn't going to be my type," Grace says.

Later in the week, Grace started talking with some girls in her French class. "They seemed friendly," she recalls. "They asked me to go to lunch with them and I had the most amazing time. They were really fun, really nice, and accepted me the way I was. I felt much more comfortable."

Looking back, Grace says she's glad she had that difficult experience in the lunchroom. "I learned a lot about myself," she says. "I realized that trying to fit in with people just because they're in the 'cool crowd' wasn't a good idea. I learned that it's more important to choose friends based on how they treat people. I also learned that it's always better to just be myself. That's the best way to find true friends."

When I first got to my new school, I tried to fit in with a group and it didn't work. Then, I tried to fit in with another group and that didn't work either. Things are better now. I decided the best way to meet friends is to just be myself. That's how I found a group of friends I'm really comfortable with.

—Abigail, 12

Remember Sabrina? You met her in Chapter Two. Sabrina and her family moved to a new country where many things felt different and unfamiliar. She was eager to meet friends so she could feel happier and more comfortable in her new surroundings.

When Sabrina started going to her new school, she quickly noticed three girls who always spent time together during lunch and recess. "I wanted to be friends with them," she recalls. "I wanted to fit in with them." One day, these girls invited Sabrina to join them in the playground. Sabrina was thrilled. However, her excitement didn't last long. She noticed these girls talked a lot about the kind of clothes they were wearing, like which brands they liked the best. They also spent plenty of time talking about their favorite stores in the mall. Every day for a week, they spent most of recess talking about clothes and shopping.

"I care about what I wear," Sabrina explained. "But it was hard to just talk about clothes. I thought to myself, 'This is so boring. Why am I talking about this?'" That's when Sabrina made an important discovery. Making friends and fitting in may feel a little strange, at first. After all, it takes time to get to know new people and to let them get to know you. However, you should feel comfortable and able to be yourself when you're together. "If you try to fit in with people and it doesn't feel right, you may be trying to fit in with them every day for the rest of the year," she explains. "That's a lot of work!"

As Grace and Sabrina discovered, fitting in doesn't necessarily mean trying to be part of some "in" crowd. The only crowd that really matters is the one you create with guys and girls you trust and feel comfortable around.

What's more, fitting in doesn't involve trying to change who you are in order to make others more interested in you. In fact, the best thing you can do is be yourself. When you let others get to know the real you, you'll be more likely to develop lasting friendships. Even if it takes a little longer to find the right friends for you, hang in there. Chances are, you'll be glad you did.

CASTING CALL How Well Do You Know Your True Self?

Put a check-mark next to the situations where kids are staying true to themselves. Put an X next to the ones where they might be trying to change who they are to fit in and may have a tougher time meeting true friends.

_____ **Kira** develops a friendship with a guy who's a big science fiction fan. She smiles and tells him she doesn't know the difference between an alien and an asteroid. As they get to know each other, they find they share plenty of things in common. She also learns all kinds of new things about far-away galaxies.

_____ **Zach** starts hanging out with some boys who want to play video games every weekend. He likes video games, but wants to do other things, too. Instead of suggesting a game of basketball or a movie, Zach decides to keep his wishes to himself because he's afraid he'll lose their friendship.

_____ **Mariam** notices that many of the kids in her new school seem to go to the same place to get their hair cut. They all wear the same hairstyle! Even

Put Your Best Foot Forward

In Chapter Five, you read about the importance of getting to know people before judging them too quickly. The old saying, "You can't judge a book by its cover" still holds true. However, when people don't know you yet, they may look for clues about whether you're interested in meeting them and whether you might share some common interests or values. That's where first impressions can come in handy. The first rule of

though she likes her super-curly hair the way it is, she decides to change it so she can look like everyone else.

_____ **Paulo** is interested in meeting new friends so he tries out for the school chorus. He has a great voice and he's always loved to sing.

_____ **Neal** sits with a group of kids at lunch who start saying rude things about other people. He decides to find other people to sit with tomorrow.

_____ **Alison** would like to get to know a girl in her science class. She decides to tell far-fetched stories about herself—like saying she's the cousin of a super-famous Top 40 singer—hoping that'll make her classmate more interested in starting a friendship.

Answers:

Kira, Paulo, and Neal sound like kids who stay true to themselves and are more likely to feel comfortable with the friends they make.

Zach, Mariam and Alison sound like kids who feel the need to change their personalities or interests in an effort to fit in. This behavior will likely make it difficult to feel good inside, and harder to meet friends they'll trust and enjoy.

making a good impression is that there are no hard-and-fast rules! As long as you strive to be yourself and treat others the way you'd want to be treated, you're well on your way to putting your best foot forward.

Here are some dos and don'ts to help you get started.

Three Dos:

* **Be approachable.** Pay attention to your body language and your attitude. If you're sitting at a table looking down and avoiding eye contact with others, it may send the message that you don't want to meet people. On the other hand, if you're looking up and smiling, this lets people know you're interested in getting to know them.

* **Be friendly.** Show a genuine interest in the people you meet. "It's better to take an interest in others than to talk about yourself too much," advises Aaron. "People like it when you want to get to know them." Also, be open to getting to know all kinds of friends, rather than believing that there's only one "type" of friend for you.

* **Be yourself.** It's natural to want to fit in, but be sure to stay true to yourself and your values. If, at first, you don't meet people who accept you as you are, keep looking.

Three Don'ts:

* **Don't be dishonest.** It may be tempting to tell false stories about yourself to try and impress people, but resist the urge. "You may think people will like you better if you say you're really rich or you visited a bunch of countries, but they'll eventually find out and think you're not an honest person," says Luke. "Just be yourself, and you'll find friends who like you for who you are."

* **Don't be a gossip.** Some kids think that if they talk negatively about others, it might make them appear more popular or interesting. Talking about people behind their backs is not nice, and it's not a good way to make friends—or a good first impression. It may be tempting to say mean things, especially when the people you want to be friendly with are doing it. Even if this seems like an easy way to form new friendships, it can hurt feelings.

* **Don't be pushy.** It's one thing to be friendly, but it's another to try and push a relationship too quickly or try and get in the way of an existing friendship. If you're getting the feeling that someone's not ready to make plans with you every weekend or eat lunch with you every day, take a step back and let the relationship develop over time. Meanwhile, be sure to seek other friends so you don't focus on only one or two people.

> It was kind of fun to start over. I thought about how I wanted people to see me. First, I wondered if it would be cool to talk with a British accent! Then, I thought I would wear glasses, even though I didn't need them. I decided against the fake accent and the glasses because that's not who I am. I just decided to be myself and if people didn't like me for who I was, then they probably wouldn't have been the right friends for me.
>
> —Hannah, 14

> You can't push your way into a group. Don't always talk. Sometimes, it's better to listen and not interrupt conversations. It's hard, but you have to wait until people are comfortable with you and you're comfortable with them. Friendships don't happen overnight.
>
> **—Maddie, 14**

Even when you put your best foot forward and try some of the dos and don'ts listed above, you're not going to develop friendships with everyone. It wouldn't be realistic to expect that you'll become close with every person you meet! If someone doesn't feel right for you, that's okay. Keep your eyes open for the next person.

Try New Things in New Places

As you've read, it can be uncomfortable and dishonest to pretend you're someone you're not just to make new friends. However, if you stay true to yourself, it can be fun and interesting to make some positive changes in your life when you meet new people. That's what Maddie did each time she and her family moved due to her father's job. "Because I moved so many times, I started to think of it as a chance to start over and be something even better than I was before," she says.

Reinvent

(verb): to do something differently from before, especially in order to make improvements.

Maddie has many wonderful qualities to be proud of. She's a loyal friend, a hard-working student, and a kind and thoughtful person. Yet, she says it's always fun to set a new goal or experiment with a slightly different type of personality when she moves because no one knows what she was like before. "In my old school, I was a little quiet and shy and afraid to be myself around other people," she explains. "When we moved, I decided I was going to be myself around everyone and not be so shy. It was fun to reinvent myself a little."

While it can be fun to challenge yourself to grow in new ways or explore a new side of your personality, it's important to stay true to yourself and your values. There's a big difference between changing your behaviors and changing who you are. For example, if you start hanging out with new friends who pressure you to do something you're uncomfortable with—like trying drugs or alcohol, skipping class, shoplifting, or taking other risks—take a step back and think about your decision. Peer pressure can be hard to resist. When you are eager to fit in, you might feel tempted to go along with a crowd. However, it's important to stick to the behaviors (and the friends) that feel right for you and help you stay happy and safe. It takes courage and strength to resist negative peer pressure and stay true to your values. When you do, you'll feel good about yourself and your choices.

What's Your Friendship-Making Style?

Choose true or false in response to the following statements about meeting new people.

T/F When I meet someone new, I'm interested in getting to know them. I'm also eager to share things about myself and my interests. I want them to meet the real me.

T/F When I start to hang out with a new group of friends, I understand that it may take some time to really get to know each other.

T/F I'm not going to develop friendships with everyone I meet, and I'm okay with that. As I get to know new people, I'll start to notice the ones that feel the most comfortable to me.

T/F When I think about my closest friends from my last school, I remember that we didn't rush our relationships. Some of our most meaningful "best friend" conversations took place after we really trusted each other.

 Plot Summary

Chapter 6 was all about finding ways to fit in without rushing into new friendships. You learned that fitting in doesn't mean trying to change your personality or become someone you're not. It's about being true to who you are, and finding friends you feel comfortable with and trust.

T/F It can be fun to meet new people, even if they don't like all the same things that I do. I can still be myself, and I might get to discover new interests and activities I never experienced before, like playing a new sport or listening to a new band.

T/F It would be great to have instant friends, but I know I might need a little time to figure out which guys and girls would feel the most comfortable to me.

About your score:

If you answered true to four or more statements, you're open to new friendships and you're eager to let people get to know the real you. You're not going to rush things, though, because you believe that relationships take time to grow.

If you answered true to three of these statements or fewer, you may be trying to rush into new relationships too quickly. Or you might be feeling the need to become someone you're not in order to fit in. It's natural to want friends right away, especially after experiencing big changes, but take your time getting to know people and always be yourself. Keep reading for more ideas on how to get know the new people in your life.

 Coming Attractions

If you're wondering how to juggle old friendships with new ones, you're not alone. It's not always easy to stay close with friends, especially after you switch schools or move many miles away. Chapter 7 will give you tips on how to keep those connections strong.

CHAPTER 7

Juggling Old and New Friends

> I lived in one town for eight years and then another for three years. I still have one close friend from the first place I lived. We talk a lot. I didn't really stay close with other people, though. You always say you'll stay in touch with everyone, but it's hard. I'm pretty busy now.
>
> **—Malik, 12**

> Dealing with old and new friends was probably the hardest part of switching schools. My old friends were pretty upset that I was leaving and I didn't want them to feel bad.
>
> **—Gianna, 11**

> At first, I texted and called my old friends a lot. I wanted to feel like I was there and that I wouldn't miss anything. I didn't want to feel left out.
>
> **—Hannah, 14**

**M**eeting new friends and getting to know them takes time. So does keeping up with old friends. Between homework, sports, hobbies, and watching reality television, you may wonder how you'll have time to make new friends and stay in touch with your old ones.

Of course, juggling old and new friendships involves much more than fitting in a few "how r u?" text messages between soccer practices. It involves making an effort to reach out to old friends you care about. It involves being sensitive to the feelings of others, like new friends who may not want to hear every detail about how great your old neighborhood was, and old friends who aren't necessarily interested in the score of every basketball game you play with your new next door neighbor.

Juggling old relationships and new ones also involves being careful not to spend so much time calling old friends that you might be missing out on opportunities to make new ones.

It's certainly possible to keep friendships going strong, regardless of where you live or how much time passes between visits. In fact, your parents and grandparents may still keep in touch with childhood friends even though those relationships started long before text messaging was invented!

These days, there are all kinds of ways for you to stay connected to the people you care about. You can call, visit, text, chat online, or even communicate the old-fashioned way by sending a letter in the mail. The key is to find a healthy balance between connecting with old friends and spending time with new ones. It also helps to be sensitive to friends' feelings, and realistic about how these relationships may change over time.

Keep in Touch

Let's imagine we're listening in on a phone call between two friends, Maya and Yolanda. Maya recently moved to a new town and started a new school. She misses Yolanda and wants to keep in touch.

Maya can't wait to share her new experiences. "Yolanda and I are best friends," Maya thinks to herself. "I'm sure she wants to hear all the details of my life."

Maya: Hey. What's up?

Yolanda: Not much, what's up with you? What's it like there?

Maya: Everything's great. I've been super busy. Everyone's really nice. Oh, and I love my new school. We have the best football team. It's so much better than our old team. My new room is awesome. It's way bigger than my old one. Yesterday, I went to the mall with my new friend Kelsey and we saw this really cute dress that I'm going to save up for. You'd love it.

Yolanda: Cool. What store did you go to?

Maya: Oh, you wouldn't have heard of it. They don't have one where you are. It's awesome. There are a million great stores here. I like them so much better than our old ones.

Yolanda: Um hmm.

Maya: Well, Kelsey's at my house now and we're going to the movies so I have to talk fast. I just wanted to say hello.

Yolanda: Okay.

Maya: Gotta run. Bye.

No doubt, that phone call started with good intentions. However, it may not have ended well. How do you think Yolanda felt? Why?

Now, here's another version of the phone call between these friends.

Maya: Hey. What's up?

Yolanda: Not much, what's up with you? What's it like there?

Maya: Well, I'm meeting new people and seeing new places, but I miss my old friends. What have you been up to? What's new?

Yolanda: I've been playing soccer a lot and hanging out with Jenna and Jaime. It's not the same without you.

Maya: Thanks. Please tell them I said hi!

Yolanda: What's your new school like? Do you like it better than our old one?

Maya: I like it. We have a really good football team so it's fun to watch them play. I'm also meeting nice people so I'm glad about that. I have a new friend named Kelsey. You'd like her. She said she wants to meet you! My teachers are nice, too. But there's no one as funny as Mr. Williams. I actually miss his corny algebra jokes. Do you have him again this year?

Yolanda: No, but I wish I did.

Maya: It was great talking with you, but I have to run now. Let's ask our parents if we can plan a visit sometime soon. I want to show you around the neighborhood and take you to some fun new places. There's one store that always reminds me of you. You'd love it!

Yolanda: That sounds great. Thanks for calling. Miss you! Bye.

What about this call? How did it differ from the first? What did Maya do to help the relationship stay strong?

At first glance, the two phone calls may have seemed similar. Both were relatively short, and both took place after a recent move. However, there were important differences in the way they were handled.

In the first call, Maya talked mostly about herself and her new experiences. She didn't give Yolanda many opportunities to share details of her life or talk about things that are important to her. She also made a point of comparing her experiences, and sent the message that her new situation is better than her old one. In fact, she may truly feel this way. However, bragging is a sure way to alienate friends and hurt feelings. It is definitely not a way to maintain relationships!

In the second call, Maya managed to share information about her new school and her new experiences. However, she was sensitive to Yolanda's feelings. Even though Yolanda asked Maya if she likes her new school better, Maya managed to share her enthusiasm without saying negative things about her old school. She was also able to let Yolanda know that she's doing well and meeting new people, yet she still cares about her old friends and misses them.

> People always asked me, 'Do you like it better here or where you used to live?' I didn't want to offend them and say my old neighborhood was better. But I didn't want to say bad things about it, either. I just said, 'Um, I don't know. I'm not sure yet!'
>
> **—Janessa, 12**

Balance Old and New

Here are some ideas for keeping your old friendships strong while cultivating new ones:

* **Be sensitive.** It's okay to talk about your new school and your new friends, but try not to compare them or say negative things.

* **Be interested.** Even though you're the one who's experienced all kinds of changes recently, your old friends still have plenty of stories of their own. Always ask what they've been up to, and be sure to be a good listener.

* **Be realistic.** When you change schools or move to a new town, you probably won't stay in touch with everyone. As you meet new friends and share new experiences, you may not have as much in common with old friends as you used to. If you want to stay close with a few best friends, go for it. However, it may be unrealistic to expect that you'll maintain close relationships with everyone you've known since kindergarten. It may be helpful to remember that, even if you stayed in the same spot your whole life, friendships change over time. Do your best to stay connected with old friends, but be open to meeting new ones, as well.

 Plot Summary

In this chapter, you learned that juggling isn't just for circus clowns! Keeping up with old friends while you're making new ones isn't always easy, but it can be done. You gained new skills to maintain treasured relationships.

What's My Next Line?

Losing Touch

What if these keeping-in-touch tips just aren't enough to keep your relationships strong? You might notice that some old friends aren't calling as often as you'd like. Or you might sense that a friend or two may be envious of your new experiences, or feeling left out.

One of the best ways to take care of any relationship (whether or not it's long distance) is to communicate. You might say to an old friend who seems too busy to keep in touch, "I miss talking with you! Let's catch up soon." This next message may be appreciated by a friend who is feeling left out: "Even though I'm meeting new friends here, I hope we'll always stay close."

Communicating with friends is an important way to strengthen relationships. However, there are no guarantees that friendships will stay exactly the same. "When I told my best friend, Julia, I was moving, she was really mad," Hannah recalls. "Even though it wasn't my fault, I wanted to make things better. At first, it was hard. She kind of ignored me when I tried to call. I told her I missed her and really wanted her to visit. I also made sure not to talk about my new friends too much to her. I didn't want her to feel bad."

Today, Hannah and Julia still keep in touch. However, both girls have made new friends and are busy enjoying new experiences. "I wouldn't say we're best friends anymore," says Hannah. "But we can always call each other and, hopefully, we'll stay close."

Coming Attractions

Throughout this book, you've read the stories, successes, and stresses of new kids just like you. In the final chapter, you'll learn how to pull all this information together and create a new kid survival plan that works for you.

CHAPTER 8

Moving Forward

Like you, the girls and guys in this book have been new to a home, neighborhood, school, or all three. Sometimes, they felt worried and sad. Other times, they felt happy and hopeful. Most of the time, they discovered something new about themselves or others, and learned a lot from their experiences.

Learn for Life

In fact, new experiences can bring all kinds of new lessons. "New lessons?" you say. "No thanks. I do plenty of learning in school." Wait! Before you skip ahead to the last page of this book, take a look at some of the lessons learned by new kids just like you.

These lessons don't require a pop-quiz or a term paper, and they're probably a lot easier to remember than the square root of 625 (and may even be more meaningful!).

Nick learned . . .

- * most people are nice and want to meet new friends
- * he's enjoying his new school more than he thought he would
- * talking about his feelings helps him feel better

James learned . . .

- * it can be fun to try new things
- * to use his personality and sense of humor to meet friends
- * change can bring a fresh start

Malik learned . . .

- * most kids are pretty friendly
- * he's more outgoing than he realized
- * he's able to deal with change

Janessa learned . . .

- * being new isn't as scary as it seemed
- * her parents are helpful and supportive
- * to be herself

Gabriel learned . . .

- * most people like when you say hello to them
- * "different" doesn't necessarily mean "bad"
- * to think about the positives

Liu learned . . .

- * things aren't as scary when your family is there to help
- * there are fun things to do everywhere
- * it doesn't take too long to make a friend

Gianna learned . . .

* not to judge things before she actually does them
* her new school isn't as hard as she thought it might be
* to keep her eyes open and be open-minded about people

Hannah learned . . .

* she can handle new situations
* she's a stronger person than she realized
* change can be good

Angie learned . . .

* not to panic
* not to be afraid to ask questions
* to be friendly to everyone

Grace learned . . .

* that "popular cliques" aren't always what they seem
* that feeling accepted for the right reasons is something she values and deserves
* to listen to her instincts

Yasmin learned . . .

* it isn't hard to find things in common with others
* teachers can help kids meet each other in school
* things get better

David learned . . .

* to introduce himself and start conversations with others
* most kids are happy to make new friends and include them in their plans
* it's possible to feel worried and excited at the same time

Maddie learned . . .

* it can be helpful to set new goals and make changes after moving
* it's kind of fun to wonder what's next
* to get to know people (and places) before making judgments about them

Calvin learned . . .

* it's normal to miss the way things were
* things don't always turn out perfectly, but they can still work out
* doing stuff he enjoys (like playing sports) helps him feel good

Aaron learned . . .

* not everyone is his "type," but that's okay
* it's normal to be nervous about change
* talking with a counselor can be helpful

Abigail learned . . .

* new steps aren't always easy
* if things aren't going well, ask for help
* parents and teachers can work together to find helpful solutions

Luke learned . . .

* it's important to get to know people before deciding to be their friend
* he can keep his old friends and make new ones, too
* to be patient; things don't always happen right away

Pilar learned . . .

* teachers can help new kids feel more comfortable
* it can be helpful to observe guys and girls before approaching them
* a great way to meet friends is through other friends

Tristan learned . . .

* an optimistic attitude can make a difference
* to accept advice from people he trusts
* he can feel comfortable—even after big changes take place

Margaret learned . . .

* her parents are looking out for her best interests
* that it's important to notice how kids treat others
* if a kid in school smiles, smile back

Sabrina learned . . .

* to be choosy about the friendships she seeks
* she can find friends anywhere—even in another country
* that gravy-covered French fries are delicious

What's My Next Line?

What Have You Learned?

Now, it's your turn. Take a moment to think about what you've already learned as a result of your "new kid" experiences. Even if you haven't made your move yet, you can think about the lessons you've learned as a result of other new experiences, like starting a new grade in school or trying out for a new sports team. Chances are, you've already learned a lot. Write down three things you've learned and keep the paper or document somewhere you can look back on and remind yourself how far you've come.

Life is filled with opportunities to learn and grow. The more you learn, the better you'll be able to handle the next changes that come your way!

Look Ahead

Throughout the pages of this book, you've read new-kid stories and learned how kids like you have faced new opportunities and challenges. You've also been encouraged to think about your own situation.

Now, it's time to create a plan that's all your own so you can make the most of your new experiences.

Screenplay for Success

Act One. The camera focuses on you expressing your feelings about being a new kid. You look to your family (and other people you trust) to help you adjust to the changes in your life.

Act Two. You decide to join an after-school club so you can stay busy doing something you enjoy. "It may also be a good way to get to know people," you think to yourself. "While I'm at it, I'll keep my eyes open for guys and girls who seem to have the qualities I value in a friend."

Act Three. The scene changes to your old neighborhood or school. You miss your best friend, and decide to call and say hello. You're eager to share stories about your new experiences, but also want to catch up on what's happening in your friend's life. You're happy to keep in touch with your old friend. You're also excited (and maybe a little nervous) to meet new ones. However, you trust that new friendships will develop before you know it. The camera zooms in for a close-up of your hopeful face. "Now what?" you wonder with eager anticipation . . .

A Starring Role

Now you're the star of your own story! Even though you may not be able to choose all the scenery or predict every plot twist, you discovered there are many things you can do to make the most of your new-kid role.

With the skills you learned from this book—along with patience, support, and your award-worthy personality—you can face your new-kid situation with confidence. What's more, you'll be better prepared to handle all kinds of changes as you grow.

Remember, new situations aren't new for long. Soon, you'll likely feel "at home" wherever you are. In the meantime, you can look forward to making new friends, enjoying new experiences, and learning new things. Enjoy the show!

About the Authors

Debbie Glasser, PhD, is a nationally recognized psychologist, teacher, and writer who helps kids discover new ways to express their feelings and cope with change. She is the co-author of *The Step-Tween Survival Guide* and past chair of the National Parenting Education Network (NPEN). She also publishes an online newsletter for parents called NewsForParents.org. Debbie lives in Virginia with her husband and three children.

Emily Schenck is Debbie's daughter. Emily moved with her family from Florida to Virginia the summer before starting the ninth grade. She and her mom wrote this book together because they wanted to help new kids feel at home in their new situations. Currently a college student, Emily enjoys playing tennis, watching reality TV shows, and hanging out with friends—both old and new ones.

# About Magination Press

Magination Press publishes self-help books for kids and the adults in their lives. Magination Press in an imprint of the American Psychological Association, the largest scientific and professional organization representing psychologists in the United States and the largest association of psychologists worldwide.